Online Marketing Mindshift

5 Concepts for Success

by Tim Priebe

Introduction

I've worked with hundreds of businesses and nonprofits since I launched my company, T&S Online Marketing, back in 2003. In that time, I've seen plenty of frustrated people.

If you're anything like them, you've also experienced frustration at some point! Maybe you've already invested time, money, and resources in online marketing, and haven't seen the return you'd like. Maybe you're just getting started, but feel overwhelmed.

You've heard everywhere that your website, social media, email newsletters, blogging, and other online marketing platforms can be effective, but they're not working well for you.

If this sounds familiar, you may need an Online Marketing Mindshift!

Who is this book for?

If you fill multiple roles in your organization, then this book was written with you in mind. And if you market for a nonprofit or service-based business, then it was definitely written with you in mind.

Of course, anyone who performs or enjoys marketing may get something out of this book. Maybe you're a full-time marketer. Maybe you do marketing for a retail company. Maybe you own your own marketing company.

Yes, marketers will probably get something out of this book as well. But it was primarily written for those who wear multiple hats in their organization.

What is NOT in this book?

I hate to disappoint, but if you're looking for tactics, you're reading the wrong book. This book won't tell you how to build your Twitter audience. It won't share a sure-fire way to get more readers for your blog. I won't talk about how to turn email subscribers into revenue for your business.

Plenty of books are tactical in nature. This is not one of them.

What IS in this book?

This book contains five concepts that, if understood, will help set you up for success. Most likely, at least one of these concepts will shift your mindset about online marketing.

Don't get me wrong. You still need to invest some combination of time, money, and resources. But these five concepts can help you avoid that feeling of frustration by providing an Online Marketing Mindshift.

Let's get started!

Mindshift Concept 1
The Whole Point

Good news! The whole point of online marketing is actually pretty simple. You've probably heard this saying:

People do business with those they know, like, and trust.

I can't leave well enough alone, so I like to modify that saying a bit to fit the online marketing world and my personal philosophy a bit better:

People take action with those they Know, Like, Trust, and Value — a.k.a. KLTV.

It's that simple!

To simplify it down into an acronym, the whole point of online marketing is to get the right people to KLTV you and your organization. Not everyone, just the right people. It's both a way to avoid Shiny Object Syndrome as well as a great way to look at your Target Audience's Path through your online marketing.

How to Avoid Shiny Object Syndrome

Most people fall into one of two camps when exposed to a new online marketing tool or platform. Your response is probably either:

"Ooh! Another new marketing tool! Awesome, I can't wait to try it out!"

…or…

"Oh, brother. I don't have time to learn a whole new tool!"

Personally, my responses are half and half. But whether you're easily distracted, or dread having to learn about them, Shiny Object Syndrome is a real issue. And because of how quickly the online world changes, it's even worse with online marketing!

However, if you keep in mind that the whole point is to get the right people to KLTV you, it makes the whole decision process much simpler.

Lighting Your Target Audience Path

Whether you like it or just tolerate it, creating content is a great way to market your organization online. But how do you do so without just spinning your wheels? How do you measure and optimize your results?

KLTV shouldn't just describe how you want your audience to feel about you. It's more than that. It's actually four distinct stages you need to move your audience through.

If you're utilizing content as a part of your online marketing, you need to create a road map. That map should demonstrate how you move the right people through those stages.

Many call this a digital sales funnel, but that doesn't completely apply if your final goal of your online marketing isn't a sale. Instead, I describe it as a Well Lit Path.

Your Well Lit Path should consist of each type of content you produce, along with that content's Clear Next Step. While you may have heard this called a "Call to Action," I'm not a huge fan of that term. Clear Next Step implies less pressure on both the individual reading it, and on you as the producer of that content.

The reality is that each person can take whatever path they want through your content. But by creating a Well Lit Path, you create a process for moving the right people through the four stages of KLTV.

And each Clear Next Step is a checkpoint that can be measured, experimented with, and optimized.

Let's take a look at the four stages.

Stage 1 - Know

Show up! You need to be present online where your right people are. Maybe they're already looking for you, and maybe they aren't. Regardless, show up where they already are.

Most likely, this will include social media and search engines. But it could also include other third party websites.

You'll need to invest resources in three areas:

1. Finding out where the right people are.
2. Discovering what the best practices are for being in those places.
3. Putting those best practices into practice.

Online Marketing Mindshift

Assuming you're representing an organization, find out the right way to represent your organization on a given platform. Ask yourself some questions including:

- Will a normal account do? Or do you need to create a personal account, then an organizational presence?
- What are common mistakes you should avoid?
- How can you best set yourself up for changes on that platform in the future?
- Is this platform free, or should you invest some money in it?
- What is available to track the effectiveness of this platform?

Really invest time, money, and resources to be sure you get the best start possible.

Stage 2 - Like

As people begin to interact with your organization online, you want them to like you and look forward to hearing what you have to say.

Ideally they'll move to reading your longer form content, including the following:

- Blog articles
- Ebooks
- White papers
- E-courses

And hopefully they'll start opting in to your content, which could mean:

- Subscribing to your email newsletter
- Liking you on Facebook
- Following you on Twitter
- Subscribing to your podcast
- Connecting with you on LinkedIn
- Subscribing to your YouTube channel

But for any of those to happen, you need to actually show personality! As much as I like robots, you shouldn't sound like one online.

You've probably seen an organization's Facebook Page, Twitter account, or even email newsletter that was nothing more than a non-stop stream of promotional updates:

"We're running a special right now!"

"We can provide this great service or product!"

"Look at us! We're great, and you should do business with us!"

That doesn't work! Or even if it does, it could work way better with a different approach.

It's called "social media" for a reason. Most people are there to be social! And even if they're not, they are looking for what's in it for them. An overwhelming majority of people don't go online specifically to see advertisements.

So show personality, have conversations, and demonstrate that you want to help people whether they can afford to pay you or not. And that will help them start to like you.

Stage 3 - Trust

Trust comes from consistency. Or, to be more precise, it comes from consistency over a period of time.

Put yourself in this situation: You've just boarded an airplane. It's a small, single propeller plane, so you're a little nervous. Then, you find out it's the pilot's first flight.

Feeling much trust?

What about this? You've just boarded the same plane. But it's not your first time. Then you find out the pilot is the same one you've flown with a couple dozen times in the past.

You're a little more trusting, right?

In online marketing, being consistent over time can apply to the following:

- The type of content you share
- The tone or "voice" of your organization
- Your publishing schedule
- How often you check in on different platforms

But just like in the pilot example, building up trust online is usually not a quick process.

I compare the trust-building process to walking a tightrope. You start on one side, heading toward complete trust on the other side. It takes a lot of careful, intentional steps to get all the way across!

Thankfully, one misstep in your online marketing is highly unlikely to result in a plummet to your death. But it may mean you have to start over again building up trust. And it may be with just one person. But because of the public nature of much of the online world, one mistake could mean restarting with multiple people!

Stage 4 - Value

The final stage? Value! This is where people will actually take the action. Depending on your goals and organization, it could include:

- Buy your products or services
- Attend a class or workshop
- Make a donation
- Volunteer

And it doesn't have to mean doing those things themselves! Someone who can become a customer, donor, or volunteer is great. Someone who can't, but can refer 10 other right people is even better!

But in order to get people to this final stage, you'll need to share a little bit about what you actually do. While you don't want to be constantly promotional, occasionally share and mention:

- Your products
- Your services
- Testimonials and reviews
- Case studies

Of course, everything in moderation. Wayne Breitbarth, a LinkedIn expert and author of the book "The Power Formula for LinkedIn Success," recommends just one out of every ten updates you post there should be promotional, and that's a pretty good rule of thumb.

Greatly Simplify Decisions

If you really embrace it, the concept of KLTV can make decisions much easier for you. When a new online marketing tool or platform pops up, just ask yourself:

"Will using this help the right people Know, Like, Trust, and Value my organization?"

If the answer is not a resounding "Yes!" then consider carefully whether investing your time, money, and other resources is worth it. After all, you want to avoid Shiny Object Syndrome.

Mindshift Concept 2
The Right Order

I've got bad news, but you've probably already figured it out for yourself: Even if you enjoy it, online marketing can be frustrating!

One huge source of frustration is actually fairly obvious once I explain it. However, if you're like most people, you've failed to see it for yourself. You may be doing your online marketing in the wrong order!

Many activities can lead to frustration if done in the wrong order, and online marketing is no exception. Many people I work with feel social media, email marketing, blogging, or other online marketing activities aren't working for them. But when we really dig in, we discover they have been trying to make it work out of order.

Think about assembling furniture. If you're like most people, at some point you've bought a piece of furniture you then had to assemble. Can you imagine trying to put it together by reading the instructions backwards? Or doing step 3, then 1, then 4, then 2, and finally 5?

It would be a disaster! It's no wonder people get frustrated when they don't know the correct order for their online marketing steps.

Let's take a look at the five steps you need to perform in the correct order to avoid that frustration.

Step 0 - Build Your Plan

Just getting on a given online marketing platform isn't a plan. It doesn't matter if it's getting on Twitter, starting a blog, or something else entirely. You need a real plan!

Now, you may be the type of person who over-plans. In that case, it's important not to get stuck on this step. But if you're more like me, you tend toward a ready-fire-aim approach.

Either way, here's a simple guide for building your plan. It can help those of us whose natural tendency is not to plan, as well as those who can get stuck in the planning step.

1. Set a Business Goal

What do you want to accomplish with your online marketing? Do you want leads? Do you want to cut down on phone calls asking for information? Do you simply want to look better or be more visible than your competition?

Whatever the case, determine what your Business Goal is.

And yes, I did say "Goal" in its singular form, not plural. Of course, you can have multiple Business Goals for your online marketing. But the fewer goals you have, the more focused your online marketing can be. So in an ideal situation, you would have just one.

Online Marketing Mindshift

2. Track Online Milestones

Naturally, you need to track your progress. The best way to do that is to set Online Milestones that tie back to your Business Goal.

You may have heard of SMART goals. Well, in this case, we want SMART Online Milestones:

- Specific
- Measurable
- Attainable
- Relevant
- Time-Bound

For example, one million email subscribers within six months is Specific, Measurable and Time-Bound. It may be Relevant to your Business Goal as well. But for most, it's probably not Attainable.

Your Online Milestones need to have all five of those attributes! If you're not sure whether they do or not, just do a little research on your Online Milestones. Is one million Twitter followers in one year attainable? Is doing a weekly email newsletter for six months actually relevant to your Business Goal?

To do your research, you can search online, or ask someone with more experience on that particular platform than you. He or she could be an online marketing expert, but could also just be another person doing online marketing for an organization.

3. Block Out Time

It's entirely possible your full-time job is online marketing. But most people have other job duties as well. It's likely online marketing is one of the first to-do items to throw out when your schedule gets hectic.

Believe me, I understand!

You need to actually block out time on your calendar on a regular basis for online marketing. Then be sure you keep those appointments with yourself.

Step 1 - Build Your Platform

It's important you know who your audience is — more on that in Mindshift 5 — find out where they are online, and then build your platform there. This doesn't literally mean recreating a website like Facebook. It just means establishing a presence there for your organization.

Of course, it's a good idea to have at least a minimal presence on all major platforms. That could include:

- A business page on LinkedIn
- A page on Facebook — as opposed to just a personal profile
- An account on Twitter
- A Google Plus page
- A YouTube channel

- A MailChimp email newsletter
- A website with a blog

However, you need to make sure it's sustainable. For example, it's better not to have a blog at all than to have one that's months or years out of date. I've talked to many people who admitted they would question whether such a business was even still around!

And be sure to invest time and/or money in building it. Don't just set it up as quickly as humanly possible, and then call it good.

Twitter is a great example of this. You can set up a Twitter account in a matter of minutes. I've done it in just a couple minutes myself, and most people I talk to say it took them far less than 30 minutes. But was it set up well? Probably not.

Rather than rushing through the setup of any platform, research current best practices and implement them. Don't get caught up in being perfect, but invest resources including time and money when setting it up. It will be worth it.

Step 2 - Build Consistency

This is the step many find challenging. The initial planning and building of your platform can be declared complete at some point, at least for a time. But building consistency really takes time.

But this is huge! It's how you end up building that Trust we talked about in Mindshift 1.

I've talked with many business owners who heard about a social media platform, set up a new account, messed around with it for a few days, then never touched it again.

That may be fine if you're just playing around with it on a personal basis. But from a business standpoint, that's not good! It can make your organization look wishy-washy and unprofessional. Again, if someone finds an inactive account for your business, how do they even know if you're still open for business?

Be consistent with your activity to establish a professional looking presence!

Here are two big tips for consistency in your online marketing:

1. Preschedule content.

You can — and should — post some of your content live, spur of the moment. But for maximum consistency, pre-schedule all the content you can get away with. This allows for inconsistency in your creation process, while the publishing of the content is still consistent. So theoretically, you could wait until the fourth week of the month, write all your content at once, and pre-schedule it to go out consistently throughout the following month.

2. Plan on setbacks.

Believe it or not, everything doesn't always go as planned! Don't schedule the minimum amount of time to get it all done at the last minute. When you block out time, schedule it well before you need it, and block out more time than you think you'll need.

One common setback is to decide an online marketing platform isn't worth the investment of time or money, but after only spending a few days or a single month using it. Be consistent over a period of time, at least 3 - 6 months. Give it a chance to really succeed. Or fail!

Step 3 - Build Your Audience

Once you've been consistent for a while, it's time to start building up your audience full of Target Audience Members.

Sure, you may have gotten friends, co-workers, and even family to connect with you already. I call those "pity likes." But are all those people Target Audience Members? Probably not.

After a couple months of consistency, you need to start attracting people who don't already know about you and your organization. Or maybe they do already know about you, but haven't been engaged in a while. Perhaps they did business with you in the past, or donated, or volunteered. But they're not actively involved now.

There are two major types of audience-building activities:

1. Macro-building

This is when you try to add a lot of people to your audience at once. It often takes the form of a giveaway, or maybe an exclusive offer or digital download for people on a particular platform.

If you've ever subscribed to the email newsletter of a retailer, you've probably received emails with deals or sales that are exclusive to subscribers. If they let you know about that in order to entice you to sign up in the first place, that's a Macro-building method.

Macro-building tends to be less work than the second category. You're casting a wide net, and chances are you may catch some people that aren't actually Target Audience Members. Macro-building also typically requires that you invest more money, but less time, than the second category.

2. Micro-building

Simply put, this is building up your Target Audience Members one member at a time. It often requires more of a time investment than a money investment. It often involves doing something for others before you expect — or ask — them to become part of your audience.

It can be something as simple as connecting with them or their organization online, or retweeting them, or posting a glowing endorsement while tagging them. Then you simply send them a message asking if they'd connect with your organization on a specific platform.

You may ask yourself, "Self, why didn't I build my audience before I started posting / blogging / emailing consistently? Wasn't I just talking to an empty room?"

Yes, there is a bit of that empty-room syndrome, excluding those pity likes. But imagine for a moment that you started building your audience before you were consistent. Not all of your Target Audience Members will do this, but some of them would look at your inconsistent activity, and decide not to connect with you.

Step 4 – Build Engagement

Engagement is simply having two-way interactions rather than only one-way interactions. It can take the form of your Target Audience Members liking content you post, retweeting or sharing content, or actually commenting. Then you write back, and voila! It's a two-way conversation!

It's great to get to this step, because this is where everything starts to pay off! In fact, this is really where the online marketing process gives way to the sales process. Good marketing is about starting conversations, and good sales starts with having conversations.

If you want all your online marketing to pay off with engagement, you need to do the following:

- Respond when people ask questions. Definitely respond when they ask you specifically, but also when they ask questions directed at all their contacts, or at the public in general.
- Share interesting, helpful content. This should be a combination of content you create and content created by others.
- Ask questions! The more specific your questions, the more likely you are to get replies.
- Promote causes you believe in. Share information about nonprofits, or events, or sales and promotions other organizations are running. This often connects with the emotions of others, including those you're promoting. And emotion often means more engagement.

Engagement is the first step actually involving the participation of others. In case you haven't figured it out yet, you can't control how other people interact with you and your organization!

Fortunately, you can seed the engagement a bit. Feel free to contact your advocates and major fans directly, and ask if they'd participate in the two-way interaction.

You can email specific people and ask them to:

- Like, comment on, and share a specific status or tweet.
- Forward a particular email newsletter to anyone they think would benefit.
- Comment on a specific blog article.

If you really want to take engagement to the next level, build a database of your advocates and create a schedule of how often you'll ask them for help. Depending on those individuals and the level of help, you could be asking once a month, once a quarter, or just once every six months. Then track your activities and your success with those activities.

Cyclical and Ever-Changing

All of these steps are both cyclical — ongoing — and ever-changing. Back in the early 2000's, you could get away with just setting up a website, never touching it again, and being okay.

That's no longer the case!

I've heard it said when a spacecraft is on its way to the moon, it's only on the originally planned course a small percentage of the time. The rest of the time is spent making adjustments. The target doesn't change during the voyage, but the spacecraft is constantly making minor course corrections.

The same is true for your online marketing! Your goals will change. Platforms will come and go, and even the ones that stick around will change over time. You'll end up adjusting your consistency over time. And building your audience and your engagement with that audience will be an ongoing activity.

But don't work on any of the steps in this process until you've invested resources on the step before it. By doing your online marketing in the right order, you'll set yourself up for success and avoid a lot of frustration.

By Tim Priebe

Mindshift Concept 3
The Recipe for Content

Another source of frustration is your Recipe for Content. If your recipe is wrong, or you don't have one at all, it can make you feel like your online marketing is failing!

For many organizations, little thought goes into their Recipe for Content online. Instead, it looks like a mixture of randomness.

It's similar to those weird drinks kids make. When I was a kid and went to fast food places with my parents, I would get one. My kids now get one as well.

The drink I'm referring to is created by mixing in a lot of different soft drinks in a somewhat haphazard manner. It's basically whatever a kid feels like putting in there at the time.

While that drink might appeal to that specific kid right then, the same mixture likely doesn't appeal to any other kids. And it's even less likely to appeal to any adults!

In fact, a minute or two after they get it, it may not even appeal to that particular kid! It wasn't unheard of for my kids to go back, dump out their gross concoction, and end up getting a normal drink.

Maybe it's time for you to dump out your gross drink of online marketing!

Let's look at the three ingredients you can and should use in your online marketing content, using the acronym PIE. After all, the right PIE recipe is much easier to swallow than a gross drink!

- P - Promotional
- I - Informational
- E - Entertaining

Doesn't that sound delicious? Let's look at each of the ingredients.

Promotional

Many organizations consider social media nothing more than a glorified billboard when they first start out. They constantly post about their organization. Posts include deals they are running as well as products and services they offer. For some reason, it's hard for them to gain any traction, so eventually they give up.

Sound uncomfortably familiar?

Like salt, Promotional Content is great in moderation, but too much can ruin the experience for everyone.

Promotional Content is any content about you and your organization. It doesn't matter if you view it as informing rather than being "sales-y." If it's about you, it's promotional.

What are some examples?

A blog article that's a case study

You may be talking here about the benefit of working with you, and focusing on what your client got out of it, but this one still qualifies as promotional.

An email newsletter about an upcoming sale or promotion

Hopefully this one is pretty obvious. If it's any sort of advertisement, it's definitely promotional.

A social media update promoting an upcoming event you're hosting

It doesn't matter if the event itself isn't promotional at all. Any content talking about an upcoming or past event you held is promotional.

A video explaining how a service or product of yours works

Again, the lines may seem a bit blurred here. But if they have to purchase the service or product from you for the video to be of any use, then it's promotional.

Get the picture?

On the plus side, Promotional Content in moderation can move people through the Value stage of KLTV, which I mentioned back in Mindshift 1. But too much, and you'll end up pushing your Target Audience away.

Informational

If you're sharing information relevant to your Target Audience, and they can use that information whether or not they do business with you, it's Informational Content.

Informational Content is great for establishing expertise IF you focus on what's in it for the reader. If they read that content, will it benefit them even if they don't do business with you?

Let's look at some examples of Informational Content.

An ebook guide to picking a vendor

Focusing on how someone can pick an expert in your field can be beneficial, as long as it's not obviously heavily biased toward you. In fact, putting something in there about when an organization like yours would be a bad fit is a great idea.

An email newsletter with quick tips

One client of ours sends out an email newsletter with a short fictional case study each week. It's great because he's not really promoting anything, and it contains actionable advice.

Social media updates linking to informational resources

The primary strategy of many organizations on social media is to share content others have come up with. They retweet others, share links to blog articles written by others, and link to helpful resources they've found online.

A "how to" blog article

This is fairly commonplace and can be beneficial when done right. One of the most enduring "how to" articles we've written on the T&S Online Marketing website was about a specific third-party service. The company providing that service actually ended up linking to our article in their online help documentation.

Be sure to share both content you came up with as well as content created by others. Ideally, you should create some yourself. But by sharing content created by others, you demonstrate that you're focused more on the benefit to your Target Audience than you are on the short-term benefit to yourself.

Informational Content done well will help move your Target Audience through the Trust stage of KLTV.

Entertaining

Entertaining Content is intended to be completely or at least partially entertaining. Depending on your industry and organization, it may be challenging to see the benefit of content created primarily for entertainment value. If that's a challenge for you, think about content with ZERO Entertaining Content.

Nothing against lawyers specifically, but I once knew a lawyer who sent out an annual report for his clients. Talk about something with zero Entertaining Content! It was so dry, it nearly put me to sleep.

At the minimum, your content should be entertaining enough that you don't put your Target Audience to sleep.

Here are some examples of primarily Entertaining Content.

A just-for-fun video

I've seen organizations — including banks — do parody music videos. A lot of organizations have jumped on trends and done timely videos like the Gangnam style videos back in 2012 and 2013. Parody videos can do a great job of communicating company culture.

Inspirational quotes on social media and newsletters

Many people and organizations share inspirational quotes by famous people. There are even some Twitter accounts dedicated to sharing those quotes!

Thank you email blast

Many organizations send out humorous emails on occasions like holidays or their client's birthdays. Think of something you've received from a company containing a cute or funny graphic of Santa around the holidays. That was Entertaining Content.

Of course, moderation is just as important with Entertaining Content as it is with Promotional Content. Depending on your industry and organization, too much entertainment and people may not take you seriously.

And your organization may not be able to get away with completely Entertaining Content. It may not be a good fit for your organization!

However, I would challenge you to really consider creating Entertaining Content occasionally. You may find that standing out from others in your industry is a good way to draw your Target Audience to you.

Done well, Entertaining Content will help people move through the Like stage of KLTV.

Application

The whole concept of your Recipe for Content may sound great, but how do you actually apply it? With bite-size content like social media updates, you can actually determine whether each update is Promotional, Informational, or Entertaining. But with longer form content including videos, ebooks, and blogs, you can have different mixtures in a single piece of content.

Here are a few examples of how those recipes break down in both long form content as well as overall strategies for bite-size content.

Videos

My company once made a video showing a tongue-in-cheek view of what it was like to connect with us on social media. I represented my company, and one of our clients represented potential audience members.

- 10% Promotional
- 90% Entertaining

A client of ours in the training industry focuses on sales, leadership, and management training. He puts out videos explaining high level concepts that can change the way his audience thinks about those topics.

- 20% Promotional
- 75% Informational
- 5% Entertaining

Ebooks

Most ebooks are "how-to" guides, chock full of Informational Content. They usually have a few pages at the end sharing services or products the organization has available. And, of course, the ebooks should not be a dry read like that lawyer's annual report I mentioned earlier.

- 10% Promotional

- 85% Informational
- 5% Entertaining

Social Media

As I mentioned before, a LinkedIn expert I know recommends one out of every ten updates be Promotional Content. Because it's so easy to break down social media on a per-update basis, at my organization we typically just ask our clients what they want their recipe to look like. Many of them opt for roughly the same recipe.

- 10% Promotional
- 80% Informational
- 10% Entertaining

However, we do have one client who uses his social media primarily to communicate company culture. His Target Audience consists of potential employees and potential strategic partners. As a result, his recipe looks different from most other organizations.

- 10% Promotional
- 40% Informational
- 50% Entertaining

All of those recipes can be applied to other forms of online content as well. That includes everything from blog articles to podcasts, from online courses to infographics.

Regardless of your actual recipe, it's important to keep two things in mind:

1. Put actual thought and planning into creating your Recipe for Content.

2. Every organization's Recipe for Content will — and should — be different.

And the number one mistake people make with their Recipe for Content? They put too much P in their PIE. Remember, nobody likes a PIE full of P. It tastes gross.

Mindshift Concept 4
The Point of Optimization

Have you ever heard an expert in a specific online marketing platform speak on that platform? It's amazing how they tell you that your number one priority should be spending more time with that platform. You end up guilted into using it more, and probably burn out eventually.

Or maybe you've seen others in your industry spend tons of time on a specific platform, and get tons of benefit from it. You would love the same benefit, but there's no way you have that kind of time! So you don't use it at all.

It doesn't matter which of those is your issue. In both cases, the platform does you no good!

So what leads to those two problems? Is there any way to avoid them?

The key lies in understanding your Point of Optimization.

Return on Time Invested

If you enjoy math, you may enjoy this exercise. If not, bear with me for a moment and all will be made clear. If you have a piece of paper and writing utensil, feel free to actually use them. If not, your imagination is an acceptable substitute. Or you can check out the final product at ommbook.com/graph

First, draw a blank graph, with an X axis along the bottom and a Y axis along the left. Don't worry, I'll share in a moment what each axis represents.

Starting where the X and Y axes meet, draw a curved line. It should move up and to the right, then quickly begin to level off while continuing to the right. Finally, draw a dot where it begins leveling off.

Now imagine you're in a classroom full of people all drawing this graph. You look to your left and then to your right. While your graph is close to your neighbors' graphs, it doesn't match exactly. And the dot is definitely in a different spot.

I've run hundreds of people through that exercise, and have yet to find any two people whose graphs match exactly. While there have been a handful of times the lines were close, the dots were never in the exact same spot.

The Y axis is Return, and the X axis is Time Invested. The curve you've drawn — or imagined drawing — represents your Return on Time Invested. And the dot I've described is your Point of Optimization. In other words, it's the point at which you maximize your Return on Time Invested.

What does that mean for online marketing? While you could spend more time on any individual online marketing platform, it may not be worth it.

The Point of Optimization is different for every industry. It's different for every organization within an industry. It's different for every individual within an organization. And it's different for every platform one individual uses.

Just because another organization in your industry gets a lot of mileage out of a given platform doesn't mean you will. And if you're new to your job, just because your predecessor made use of a platform for your organization doesn't mean you'll get the same mileage out of it.

There are four elements that factor into your Point of Optimization.

Element 1 - Audience

How well does the audience of the platform match your Target Audience?

Some basic online research generally reveals the demographics and sometimes psychographics of that platform's users. The more in line it is with your Target Audience, the better.

Of course, it's great if they're on there at all. But the higher the platform's percentage, the better. In an ideal world, the only people on the platform would be those in your Target Audience.

For example, let's assume your Target Audience is CEOs. While there are a lot of CEOs on Facebook, most people on there are not CEOs. The ratio of CEOs to non-CEOs is much better on LinkedIn. So purely from an Audience standpoint, the Point of Optimization would be much better on LinkedIn.

Element 2 - Capabilities

How well do the capabilities of the platform match with your organization's needs?

Again, some basic online research will be revealing, and help you understand what capabilities the platform has. Some platforms have a specific focus, while others are more general.

A given platform might focus on photos, or audio, or videos, or short text posts. Other platforms will incorporate a combination of those capabilities.

For example, let's say the primary purpose of a platform is sharing photos, like Instagram or Pinterest. But your organization could have confidentiality concerns. In that case, those platforms may not be a good choice for you. Or if your product is highly visual, a podcast may not be the best idea. On the other hand, a highly visual product could be a great match for one of those photo sharing platforms.

Element 3 - Culture Fit

How closely does the platform's culture match your organization's internal culture?

An organization with an informal company culture can get more mileage out of a platform that provides an informal environment, like Twitter or Facebook. An organization with a more formal culture might struggle there.

The reverse is true as well. An organization with a formal culture would fit in on a platform like LinkedIn that has a somewhat formal culture. An organization that's informal could unintentionally give an unprofessional impression.

Have you ever seen a person or organization share something on LinkedIn that seemed like it would be more at home on Facebook? That was a mismatch on culture fit.

Of course, much more goes into an organization's culture than whether it's informal or formal. What are people there passionate about? What motivates them? Who do they admire? What are their hobbies?

Research the platform's culture ahead of time to find out if it's likely to be a match or not.

Element 4 - Comfort Level

How comfortable are you with the platform?

This is the element many experts overlook. It doesn't matter if a given platform is a perfect fit in all the other elements. If you aren't comfortable using it, you won't get as much mileage out of it.

In most cases, your comfort level will increase over time. But I've also seen plenty of cases where using a specific platform continued to be a struggle for someone. It doesn't matter how often they use it, they'll never be truly comfortable there.

That has a huge impact on their Point of Optimization!

What You Can Do

The bad news is that you can't completely know your Point of Optimization for a specific platform without investing some time using it. Maybe the capabilities looked good on paper, but you won't know if they work like you need them to without using them. Or maybe your research didn't uncover that your Target Audience was actually on the platform and fairly active. The only way to find out is to actually use the platform.

There is good news as well! You can shift your Point of Optimization in your favor, especially if Comfort Level is your biggest stumbling block.

One client of mine was using AOL to send out an email newsletter nearly every week. He usually sent out 47 a year, and each one took four hours to prepare and send. That's 188 hours a year!

We helped him switch over to MailChimp. He now spends just 30 minutes a week preparing and sending his newsletter. That means he now saves 164.5 hours a year, which is just over four work weeks!

Of course, shifting your Point of Optimization that much is pretty extreme. For you, it may just be that simply spending time getting comfortable on a platform makes a small difference, shifting your Point of Optimization just enough to make it worth it.

Regardless, the key is to not compare yourself to others. Remember the classroom full of people, each drawing graphs? The chances that your Point of Optimization lines up perfectly with someone else's is slim to none.

Mindshift Concept 5
The Journalism Questions

To avoid relying on luck, there are six questions you need to answer about your online marketing before you get started. Knowing the answers to these questions will help set you up for intentional success.

These six questions are commonly used by journalists. And if you wrote any essays in school, they may sound familiar. As it turns out, the basics of good writing also apply to your online marketing.

The six questions are:

1. Who?
2. What?

3. Why?

4. When?

5. Where?

6. How?

In journalism a story can really only be considered complete if it answers all those questions. So knowing the answer to all six questions is extremely important!

To understand why that is and how the questions apply to your online marketing, let's examine each of them one at a time.

Question 1 - Who?

Naturally, your online marketing is built to appeal to other people. If you've had any business training, you may have heard those people referred to as your ideal client, ideal prospect, or even target market. But because online marketing involves creating content, I refer to them as your Target Audience.

If your Target Audience definition starts with "everyone who" or "anybody that," it isn't specific enough.

Your Target Audience could be a number of people or groups of people, depending on the goals of your organization. It could include existing or potential people from the following groups.

- Customers and clients
- Referral partners
- Donors
- Volunteers
- Board members

- Brand ambassadors
- Employees

Most likely, you'll use your online marketing for more than one of those groups. The key is to have a clearly defined picture of who those people are and what they look like.

Of course, I'm not referring to their physical appearance, although that can be a part of it. What they look like can include both demographics — factual information about them — and psychographics — their feelings — including the following:

- Geographic location
- Their age
- Their income
- Hobbies

- If and where they go to church

- Activities their children are involved in

- The type of car they drive

- Their job

- Their budget for your products and services

- Whether they value quality, speed, or price

- How they dress

List out a handful of your favorite clients or customers, psychographics and demographics about each of them, then see what they have in common. On the other hand, you may not have any current clients you enjoy working with. If that's the case, think of real people you would enjoy working with, and start from there.

One of my clients actually named his ideal client. At his company, they talk about Molly all the time, including her demographics and psychographics, as well as whether or not she would like or benefit from decisions they make.

Now that's specific!

Question 2 - What?

Be sure you know What you ultimately want your Target Audience members to do as a result of your online marketing.

That can include the Business Goal and Online Milestones we talked about in Mindshift 2. But it may also include the Clear Next Step along the Target Audience Path we talked about in Mindshift 1.

Some examples of your What might include:

- Register for an event
- Sign up for an email newsletter
- Request a quote
- Donate online
- Make a purchase online
- Connect with your organization on social media

Regardless of your desired result, the key is to know specifically what you want your Target Audience to do.

Question 3 - Why?

Understand why a member of your Target Audience should take that action. Meaning from their standpoint, know Why they would do the What.

Sure, you may want more leads. Or maybe you want more conversations, or perhaps sales or donations. But that's making it about you, not them.

You might ask yourself:

- Does taking the action solve a pain they're currently having?
- Will taking the action provide them pleasure?
- What does their situation look like before they take the action?
- What will their situation look like afterward?
- Does taking the action help them close a gap?

This issue comes up frequently with email newsletters. The sender assumes everyone would love to receive the newsletter, but then doesn't actually provide any incentive for people to sign up or continue reading it.

Nobody cares about your email newsletter until you make it about them, not you!

Question 4 - When?

Is there a specific timeframe surrounding the action you want them to take? While this question doesn't fit every scenario, it's extremely important to know the answer when it does.

Imagine you're hosting an open house. You've already defined your Who, you know What you want them to do is attend the open house, and you're providing conversation, networking opportunities, prizes, snacks, and beverages for the Why.

At a certain point, the open house will be over, and it will be too late for people to come to the event. The When to do the What will have passed!

Other time-based promotions might include:

- A seasonal sale
- A limited time free download
- A class you're teaching
- Fundraising for a capital campaign
- Your presence at a trade show

Regardless of the specifics, online marketing for any time-based promotion has to take into account the When. Plan your schedule of activities accordingly.

Question 5 - Where?

Where does your Target Audience actually need to be when they do the What? Think both physically and virtually. The location of the desired action affects which contexts make sense for your online marketing.

Will they do the What…

- On your website, sitting in front of their computer?
- On Facebook or another social media website?
- Using a third-party website, perhaps to pay or register?
- Over the phone?
- In an app on their smart phone?
- At your physical location?
- At an event you'll be attending?

There's a reason the highway has so many billboards advertising restaurants and gas stations. They need you to drive to their location! So Where better to reach you than in your car on the highway?

In the online world, perhaps you want people to connect with your organization on Facebook. In that case, you might utilize Facebook advertising. That means people seeing your marketing are already close to Where you want them to be!

Knowing where the action needs to take place should direct where you market online.

Question 6 - How?

How easy is it for them to do the What? Even if you have great answers to the first five questions, if you screw up the How you completely derail everything.

When I speak on this topic in front of live audiences, I have an exercise that demonstrates the importance of the How.

First, I ask all the people in the audience who have ever shopped online to raise their hands. Nearly every hand goes up.

Next, I ask all the people who have ever found it challenging or painful to complete the checkout process to keep their hands up, and everyone else to put their hands down. Most of the hands stay up.

Finally, I ask everyone who has abandoned their purchase because of that difficulty to keep their hand up, and everyone else to put their hand down.

Every time, at least 80% of the audience still has their hand up!

For that purchase, the online retailer may have had all the answers to the first five questions. But it didn't matter that the audience member fit those answers perfectly. The difficulty of the How ended the transaction.

If the process of taking action is too difficult, people are far less likely to take that action.

Don't Rely on Luck

Many journalists publish stories that don't answer those six questions. And many organizations don't answer those questions either before they start marketing online. Sometimes they still luck into success.

But why take the risk? If you want the best possible chance for success, invest time in answering those six questions for your organization's online marketing.

Next Steps

While this book isn't full of tactics, there are steps you can take now. Naturally, they'll vary depending on where you currently are in the process. Here are some potential to-do items, in the order in which they were introduced in the book.

- Determine your Target Audience Path
- Evaluate your current activities against KLTV
- Build Your Plan
- Build Your Platform
- Write a month's worth of content to kick off Consistency
- Create Your Recipe for Content
- Evaluate your current activities against your Point of Optimization
- Answer each of the six Journalism Questions

Finally, while this doesn't make sense for everyone, you can also commit financial resources. Call an online marketing company to get some help.

Accountability

Want to be held accountable for your actions? Visit ommbook.com and click on "Hold Me Accountable"

What are you waiting for? Take action today!

Thank You

The material in this book was developed over the course of three and a half years. I've bounced the ideas off a lot of people in one-on-one conversations, shared it in talks with hundreds and hundreds of people, and have included the concepts in blog articles that have been read by thousands.

While I would love to thank all of those people one at a time, I simply don't know or remember everyone that's helped!

Regardless, I do want to thank a few specific people. If your name isn't in here but you contributed in some way, I definitely still appreciate your contribution.

First and foremost, thank you to my wife Leann, for supporting me in writing all the books I've put together, including this one. Love you!

Thanks to my parents for encouraging my reading and writing over the course of my life. And sometimes just tolerating it, like on those long road trips growing up.

Thanks to my kids Josh, Jackson, and Jacob, for thinking it's perfectly normal for a dad to constantly be writing books. And for interrupting me far less than they probably wanted to.

Thanks to Tracy Martino, who I believe was the first person I ever bounced any of these concepts off of back in 2012. Keep the P out of your PIE, Tracy.

Thanks to John Storm, who added Value to Know, Like, and Trust. I'm sure I'm not the only one to swipe that concept!

Thanks to Nic Bittle, who inspired the addition of Culture Fit to the Point of Optimization. Keep your shirt on in the movie theater, Nic. You know what I'm talking about.

Thanks to Tim Turner, whose constant drive to improve his online marketing led to the concept of Target Audience Path being included. Deep Space Nine is better than the original Star Trek, Tim.

Thanks to Wayne Breitbarth, author of "The Power Formula for LinkedIn Success," for recommending the specific formula of 1 in every 10 updates on social media being promotional. Thanks for coming out to Mike Crandall's facility in Oklahoma City in late April 2015!

Thanks to Matt McNeil for allowing me to use his transition from AOL to MailChimp as an example for a few years now. I swear, I mention your website every time, Matt. Case in point: okcestatesales.com

Thanks to Jay Parks for sharing with me his ideal client and how they named her Molly. I'm sure Molly loves the farm, right Jay?

Thanks to Mike Crandall, for listening to me give my talk on this topic at least a dozen times, making suggestions for improvements over the years, and encouraging me to write this book. And keeping the Critical Parent to a minimum.

Thank you to my editor, Shannon Whittington, for making great suggestions and holding me accountable for getting the book finished. Glad we're working together, Shannon!

Thanks to all my test readers: Lauren Rogers, Danna Hallmark, Hamish Knox, Phil Klutts, Carol Hartzog, and John Storm.

And finally, thanks to you. Okay, that's corny, but I appreciate your willingness to pick up this book and read it!

Want More Advice?

Frustrated with your online marketing efforts?

Worried that your online marketing isn't as good as it could be?

We have free and paid ebooks, videos, email newsletters, and more available online.

tandsgo.com/education

Connect with T&S

tandsgo.com/facebook

tandsgo.com/twitter

tandsgo.com/googleplus

tandsgo.com/linkedin

tandsgo.com/youtube